EASY PIANO CD PLAY ALONG

Volume
29

Orchestrated arrangements

A CHARLIE BROWN
CHRISTMAS™

TITLE	PAGE	TRACK NUMBER
CHRISTMAS IS COMING	2	1
THE CHRISTMAS SONG	10	2
CHRISTMAS TIME IS HERE	14	3
FÜR ELISE	18	4
HARK, THE HERALD ANGELS SING	20	5
LINUS AND LUCY	7	6
MY LITTLE DRUM	22	7
O TANNENBAUM	28	8
SKATING	31	9
WHAT CHILD IS THIS	36	10

ISBN 978-1-4234-8300-7

Visit Peanuts® on the internet at
www.snoopy.com

HAL•LEONARD®
CORPORATION

7777 W. BLUEMOUND RD. P.O. BOX 13819 MILWAUKEE, WI 53213

For all works contained herein:
Unauthorized copying, arranging, adapting, recording, Internet posting, public performance,
or other distribution of the printed or recorded music in this publication is an infringement of copyright.
Infringers are liable under the law.

Visit Hal Leonard Online at
www.halleonard.com

CHRISTMAS IS COMING

By VINCE GUARALDI

Bright Bossa

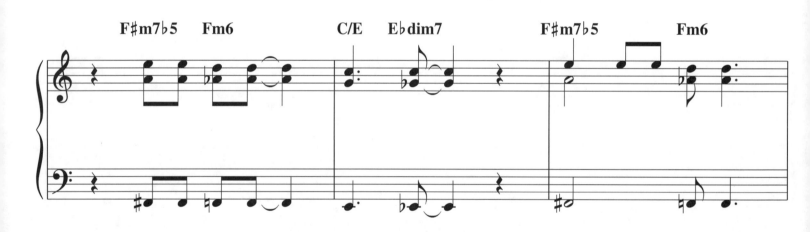

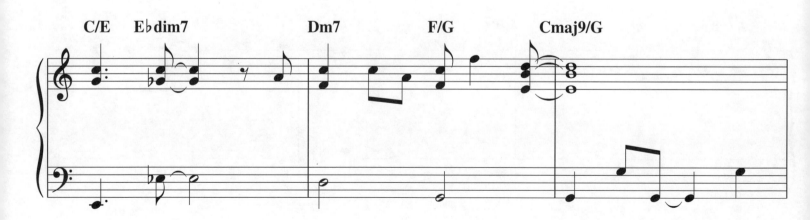

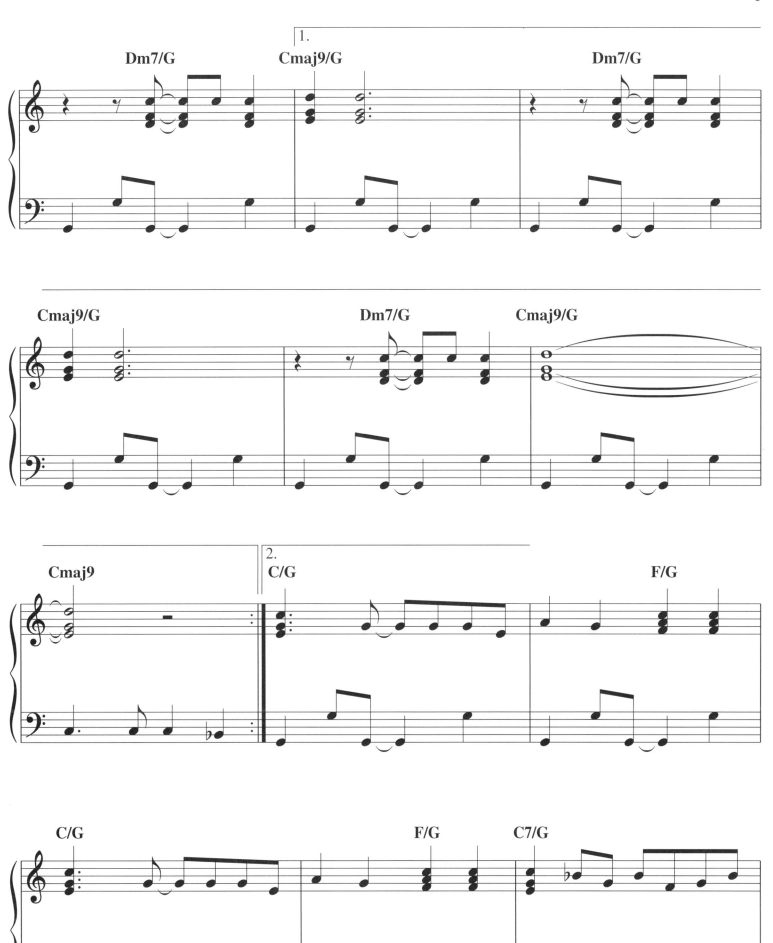

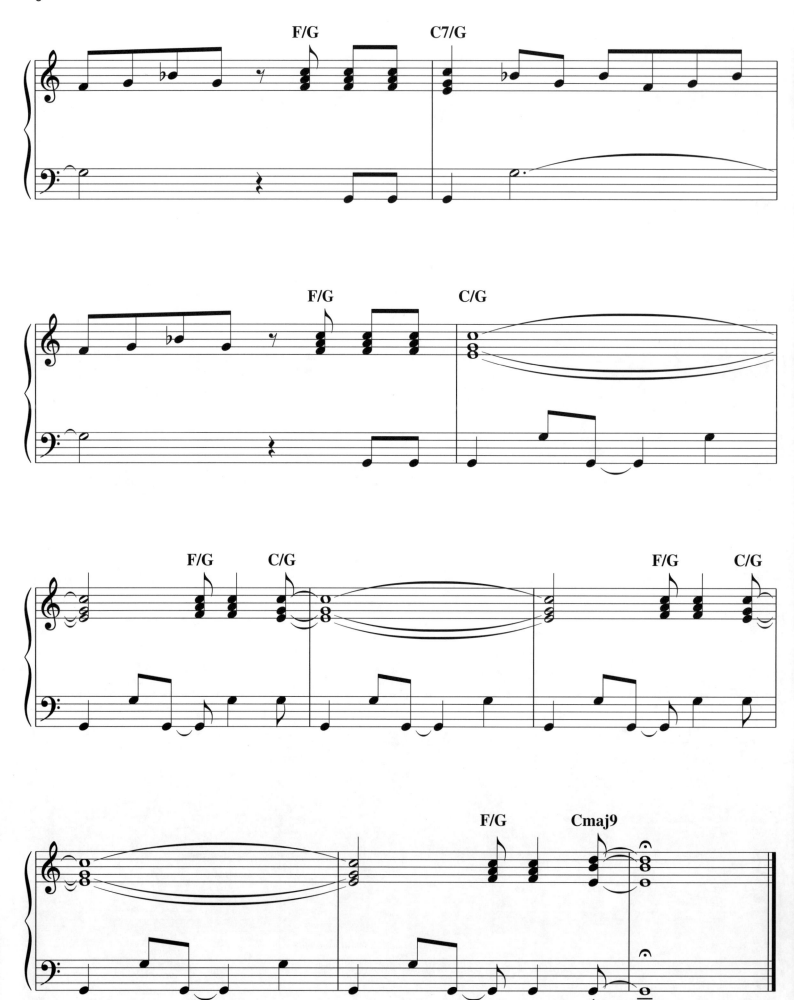

LINUS AND LUCY

By VINCE GUARALDI

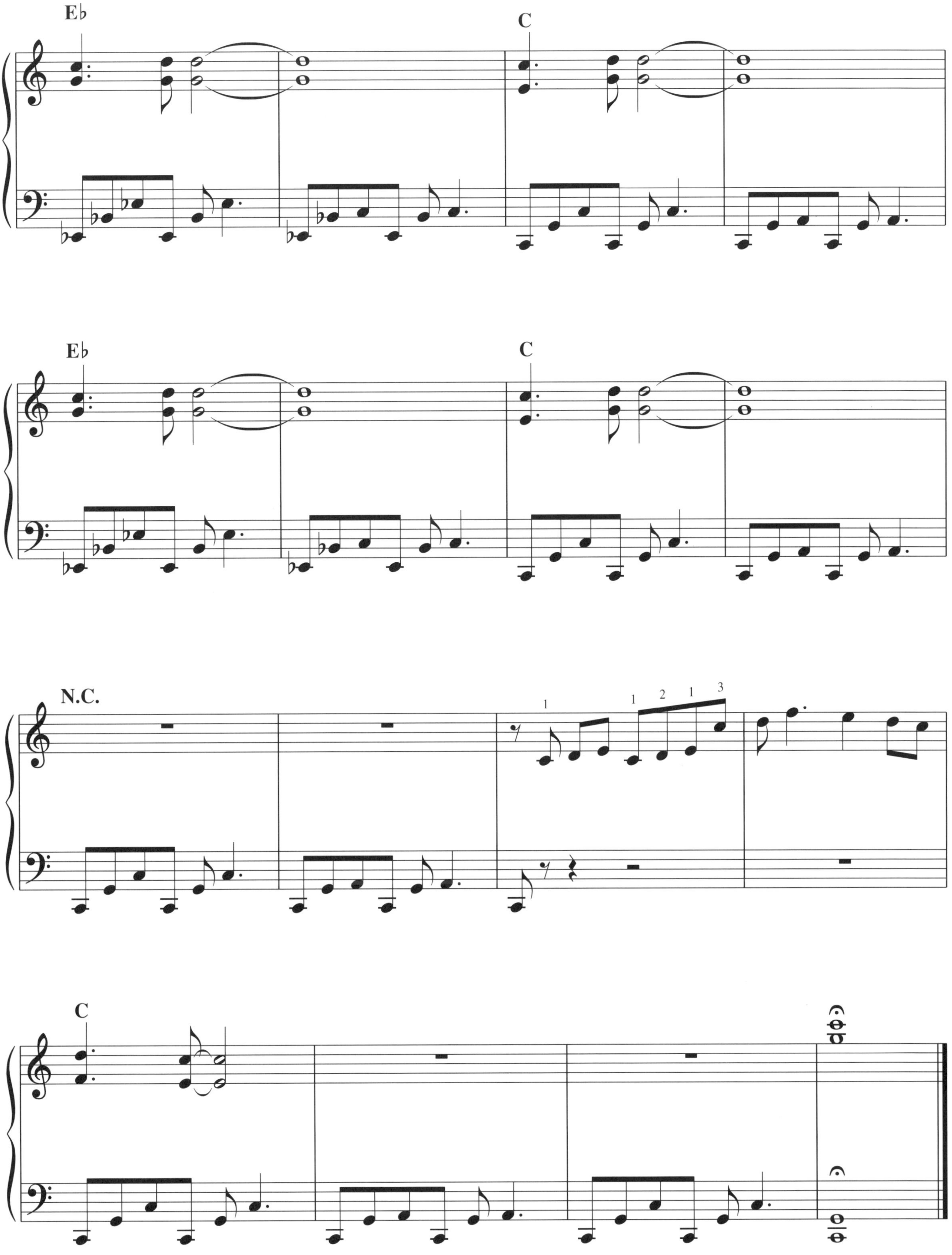
E♭
C
E♭
C
N.C.
1
1 2 1 3
C

THE CHRISTMAS SONG
(Chestnuts Roasting on an Open Fire)

Music and Lyric by MEL TORME
and ROBERT WELLS

With much expression

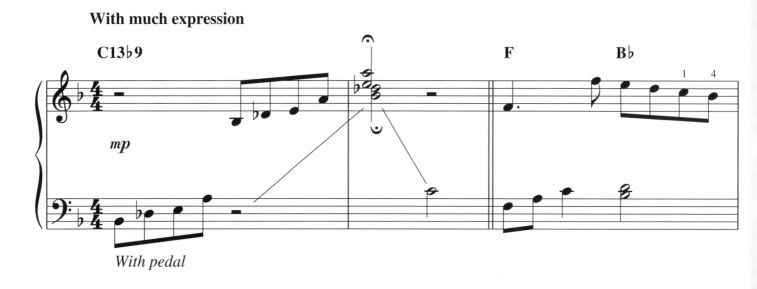

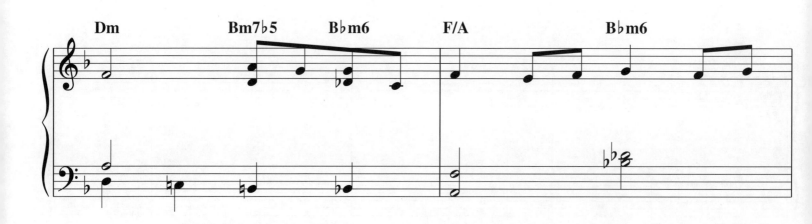

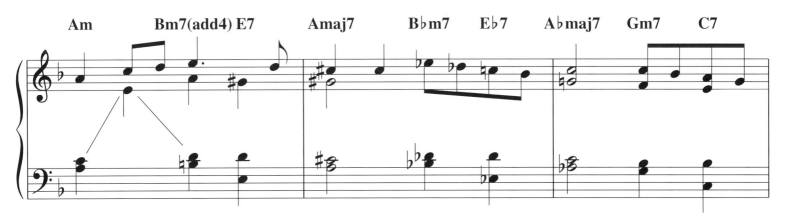

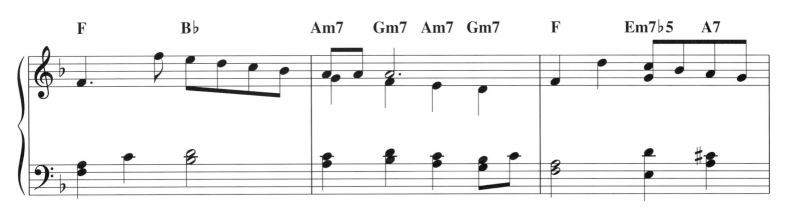

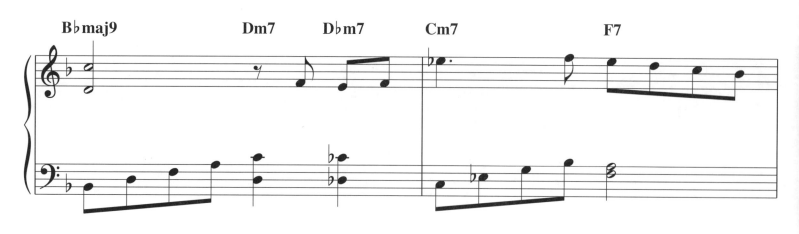

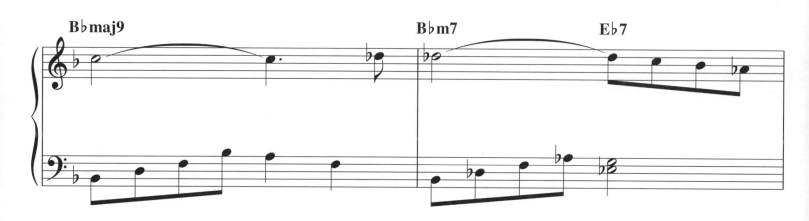

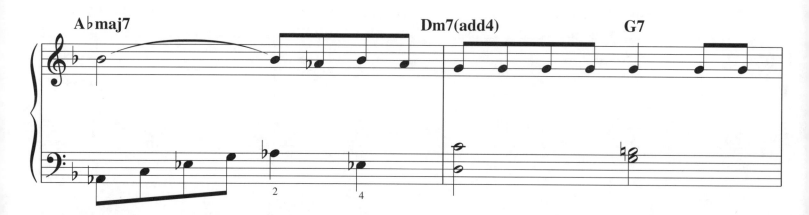

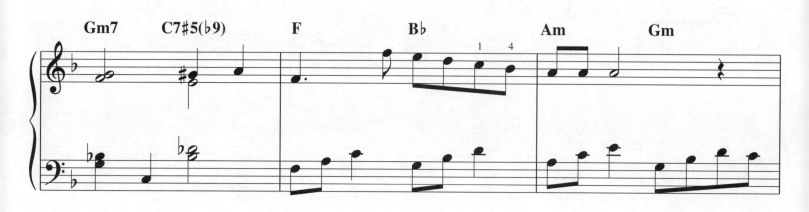

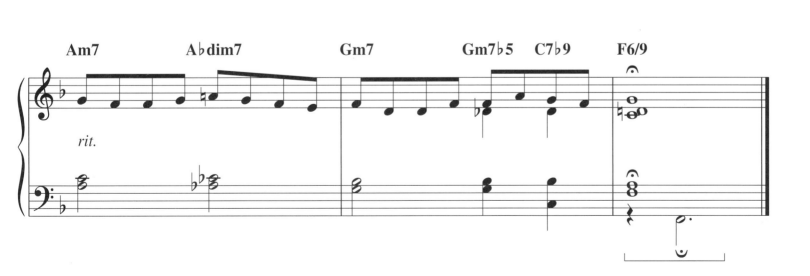

CHRISTMAS TIME IS HERE

Words by LEE MENDELSON
Music by VINCE GUARALDI

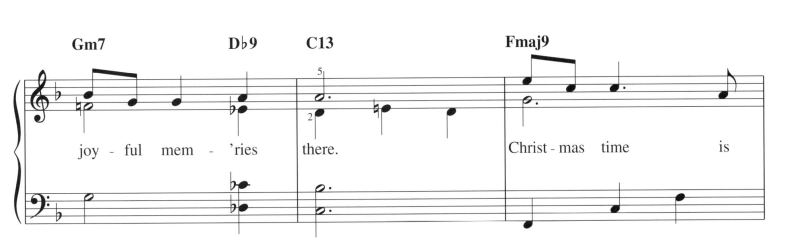

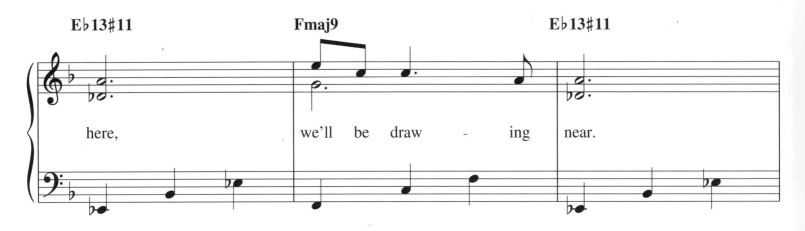

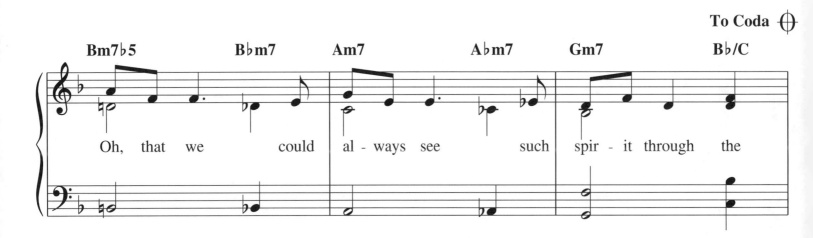

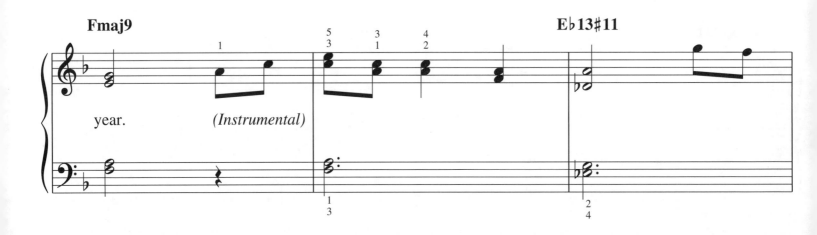

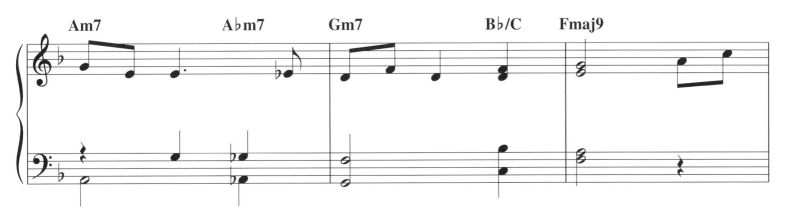

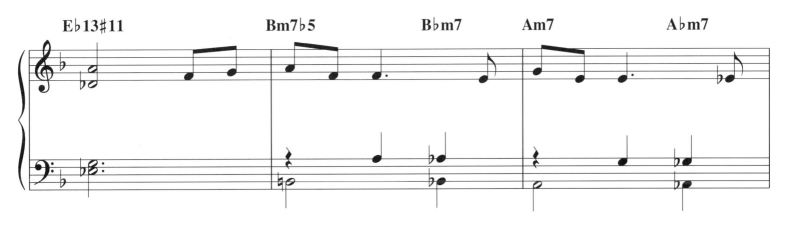

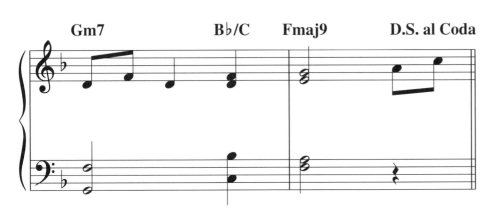

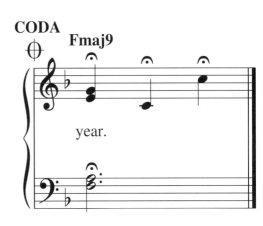

FÜR ELISE

By BEETHOVEN
Arranged by VINCE GUARALDI

HARK, THE HERALD ANGELS SING

Traditional
Arranged by VINCE GUARALDI

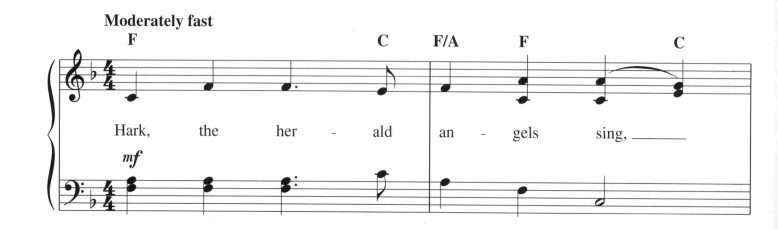

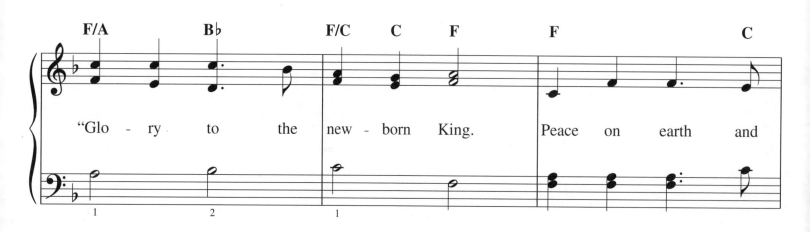

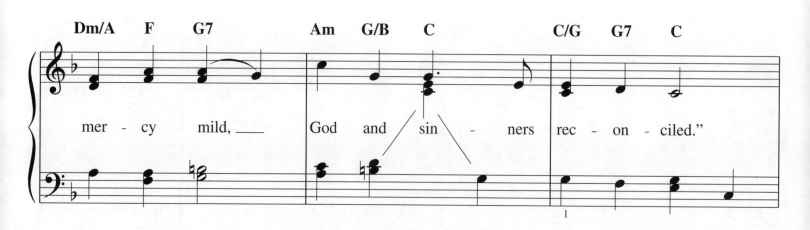

21

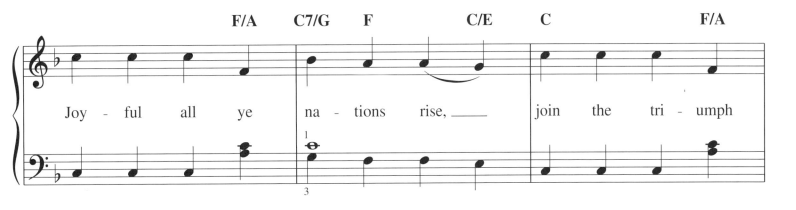

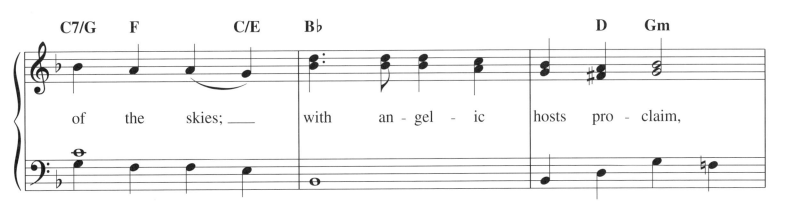

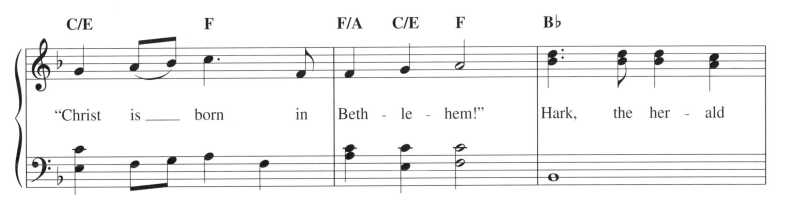

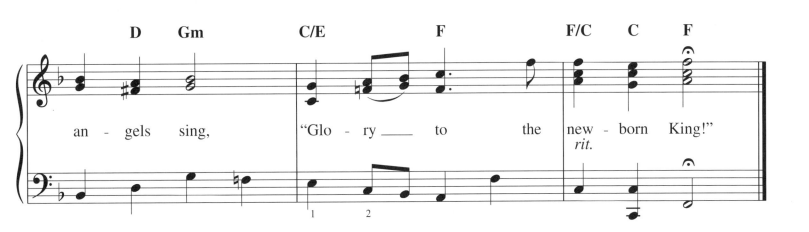

MY LITTLE DRUM

By VINCE GUARALDI

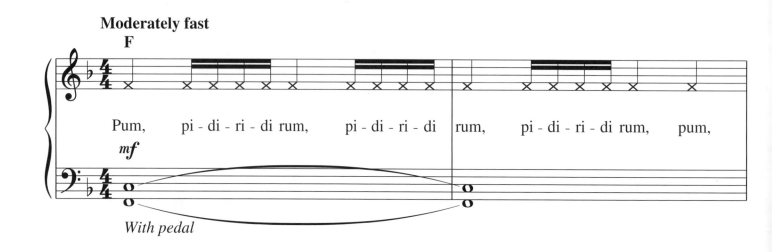

Moderately fast

Pum, pi - di - ri - di rum, pi - di - ri - di rum, pi - di - ri - di rum, pum,

mf

With pedal

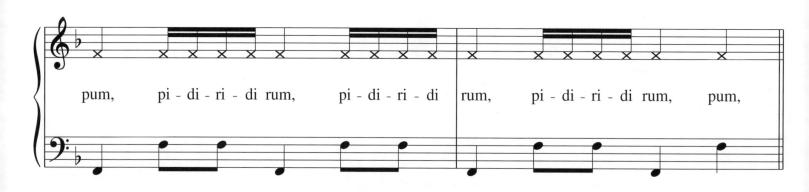

pum, pi - di - ri - di rum, pi - di - ri - di rum, pi - di - ri - di rum, pum,

(Background vocal continues)

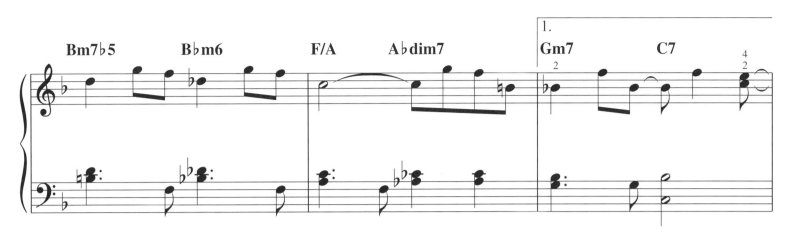

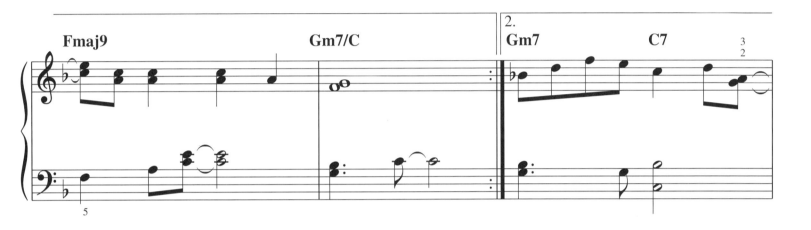

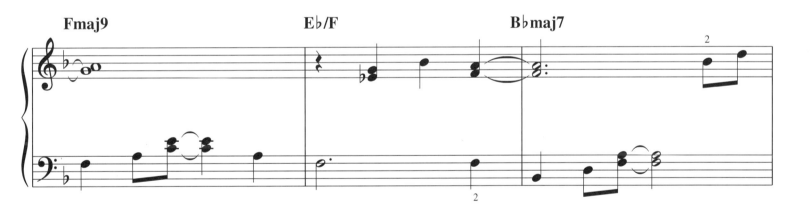

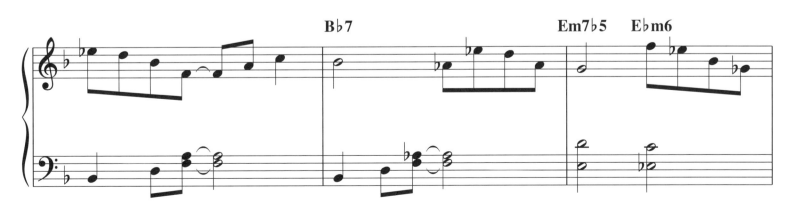

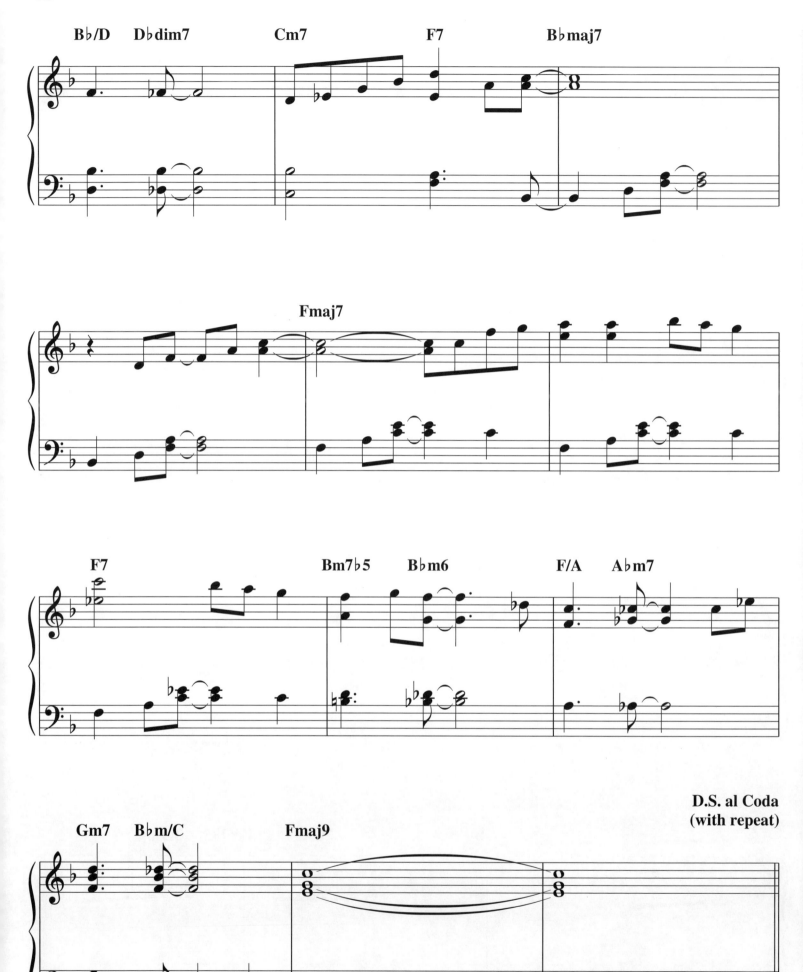

CODA

O TANNENBAUM

Traditional
Arranged by VINCE GUARALDI

SKATING

By VINCE GUARALDI

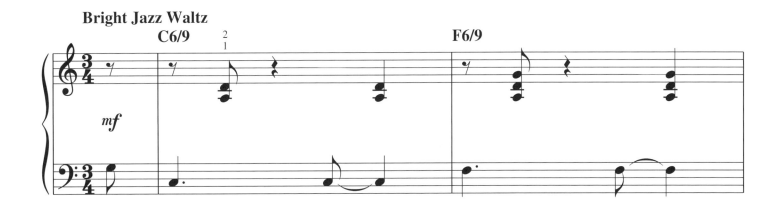

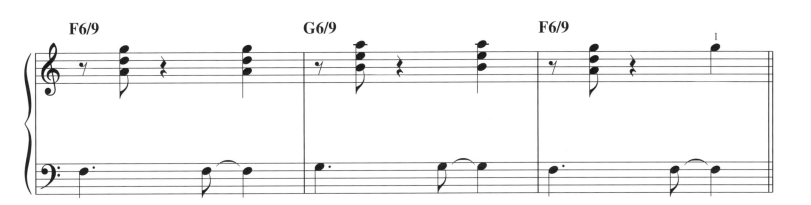

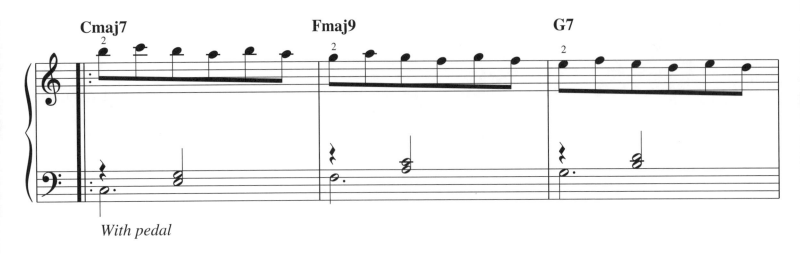

With pedal

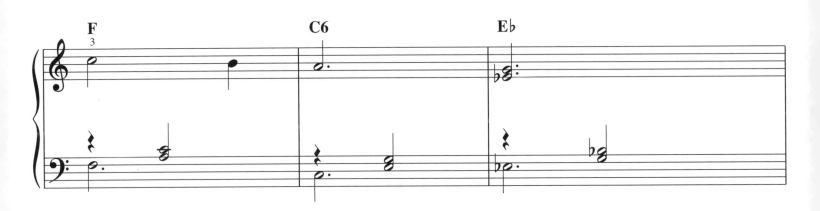

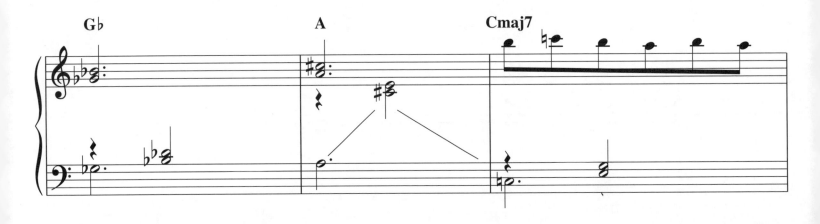

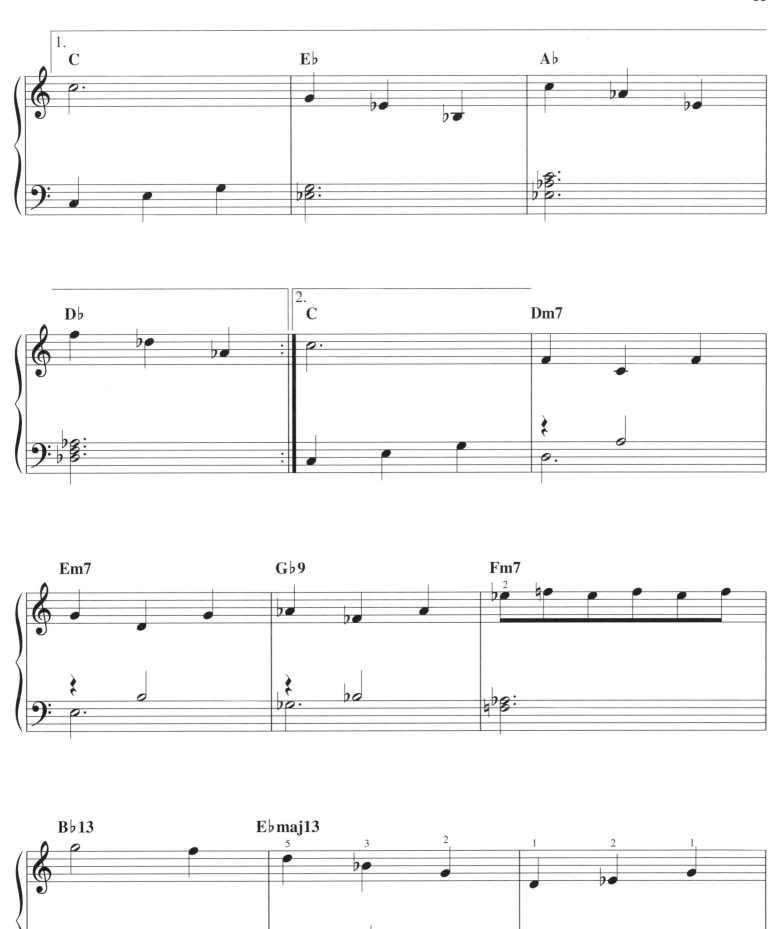

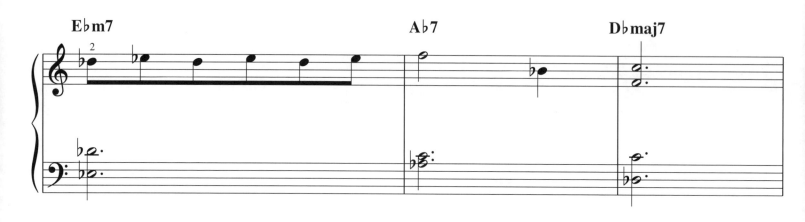

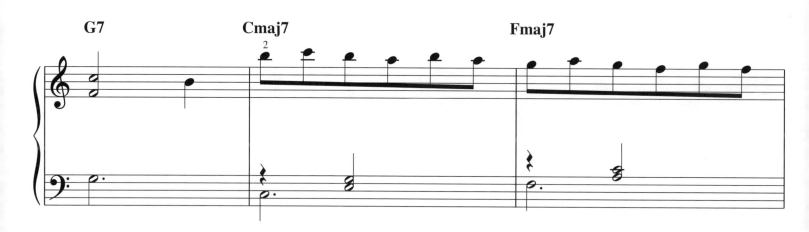

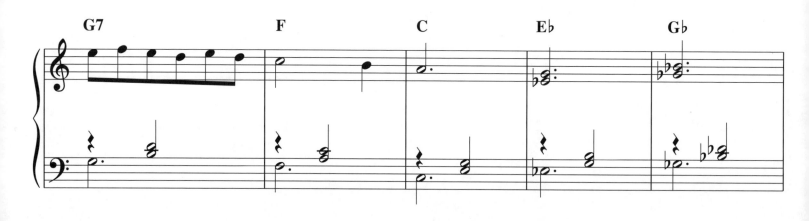

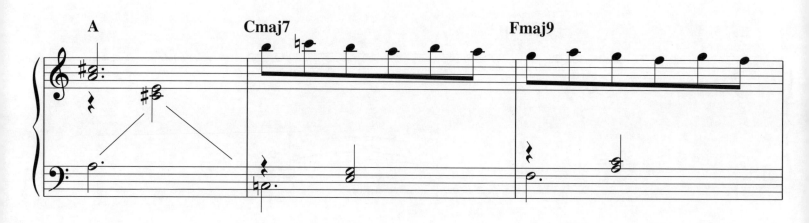

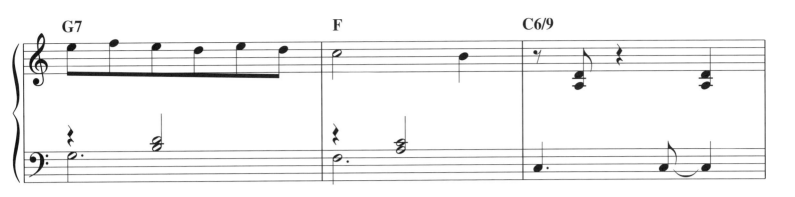

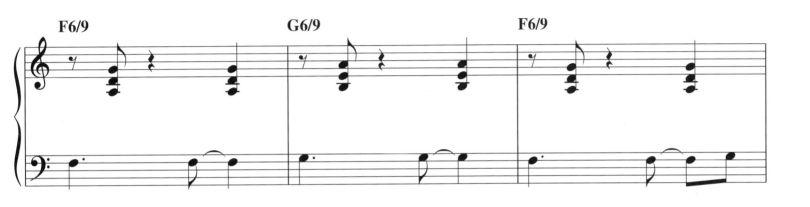

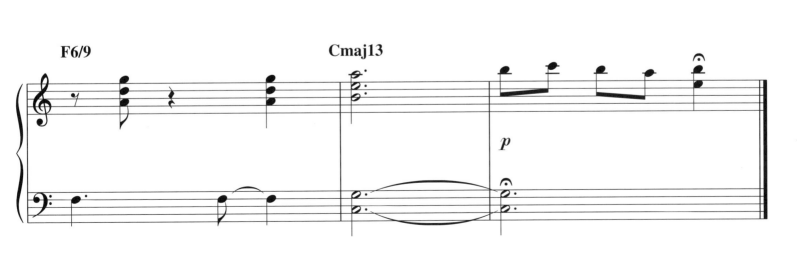

WHAT CHILD IS THIS

Traditional
Arranged by VINCE GUARALDI

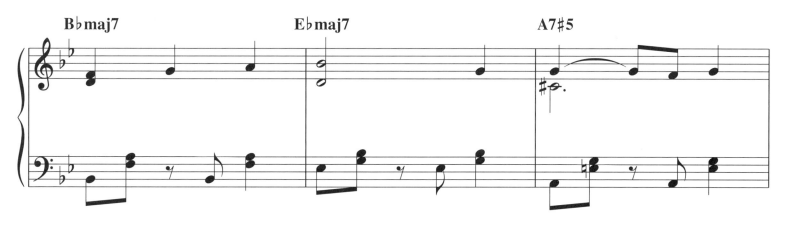

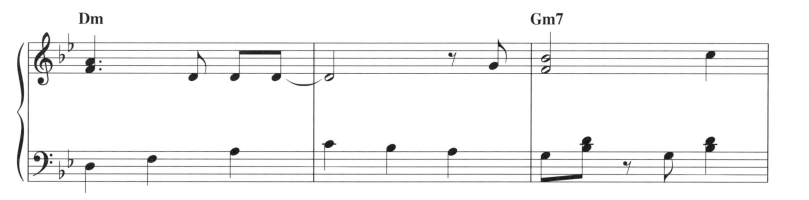

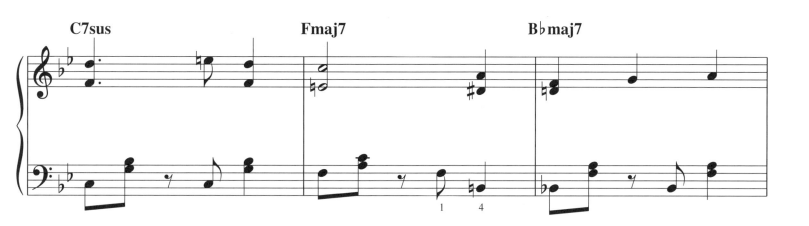

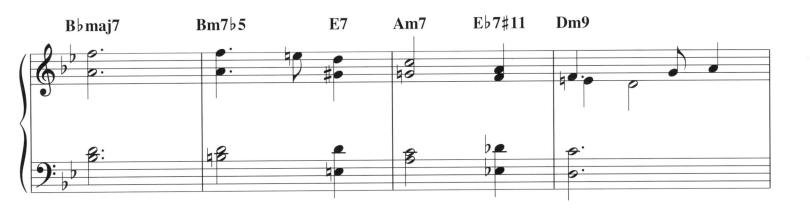

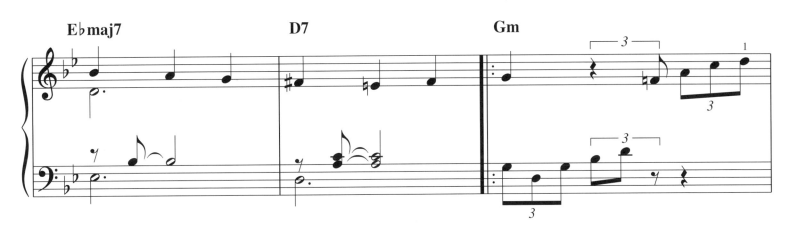

40